FOOD AND DIGESTION

Revised Edition
Steve Parker
Series Consultant
Dr Alan Maryon-Davis
MB, BChir, MSc, MRCP, FFCM

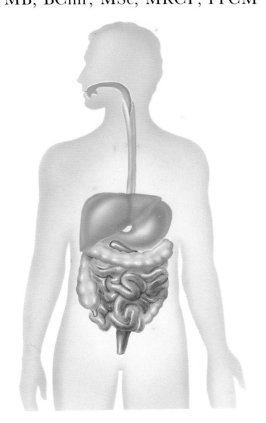

Franklin Watts
London ● New York ● Toronto ● Sydney

Words marked in bold appear in the glossary.

© Franklin Watts 1990

Original edition first published in 1982

Published in the United States by
Franklin Watts Inc.
387 Park Avenue South
New York, NY 10016

Parker, Steve.
  Food and digestion/by Steve Parker, Alan Maryon-Davis.
  p. cm. – (The Human body)
  Includes index.
  Summary: An introduction to the digestive system, discussing each
stage of digestion, the organs which aid in the digestive process,
and the assimilation of nutrients into the body's structure.
  ISBN 0-531-14027-X
  1. Digestion – Juvenile literature. 2. Gastrointestinal system
– Physiology – Juvenile literature. [1. Digestion. 2. Digestive
system.] I. Maryon-Davis, Alan. II. Title. III. Series.
QP145.P17   1990
612.3 – dc20
                                              89-36399
                                                 CIP
                                                  AC

Illustrations: Andrew Aloof, Bob Chapman, Howard Dyke,
Hayward Art Group, David Holmes, Abdul Aziz Khan, David
Mallot.

Photographs: Chris Fairclough 4, 7, 10, 18, 27, 45t; Jenny
Matthews/Save the Children 45b; NASA 20; Science Photo
Library front cover, 12, 15, 16, 21, 23, 24, 26, 28, 34, 41, 42;
Thames Water 37; Penny Tweedie/Save the Children 35;
ZEFA 8.

Printed in Belgium

FOOD AND DIGESTION

Revised Edition
Steve Parker
Series Consultant
Dr Alan Maryon-Davis
MB, BChir, MSc, MRCP, FFCM

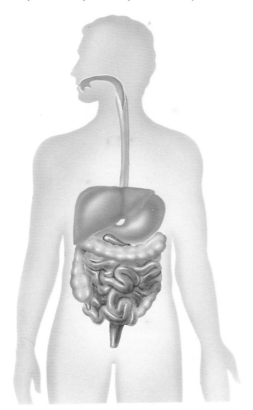

Franklin Watts
London • New York • Toronto • Sydney

Words marked in bold appear in the glossary.

Original edition first published in 1982

Published in the United States by
Franklin Watts Inc.
387 Park Avenue South
New York, NY 10016

Parker, Steve.
 Food and digestion/by Steve Parker, Alan Maryon-Davis.
 p. cm. – (The Human body)
 Includes index.
 Summary: An introduction to the digestive system, discussing each
stage of digestion, the organs which aid in the digestive process,
and the assimilation of nutrients into the body's structure.
 ISBN 0-531-14027-X
 1. Digestion – Juvenile literature. 2. Gastrointestinal system
– Physiology – Juvenile literature. [1. Digestion. 2. Digestive
system.] I. Maryon-Davis, Alan. II. Title. III. Series.
QP145.P17   1990
612.3 – dc20

                                                          89-36399
                                                            CIP
                                                            AC

Illustrations: Andrew Aloof, Bob Chapman, Howard Dyke,
Hayward Art Group, David Holmes, Abdul Aziz Khan, David
Mallot.

Photographs: Chris Fairclough 4, 7, 10, 18, 27, 45t; Jenny
Matthews/Save the Children 45b; NASA 20; Science Photo
Library front cover, 12, 15, 16, 21, 23, 24, 26, 28, 34, 41, 42;
Thames Water 37; Penny Tweedie/Save the Children 35;
ZEFA 8.

Contents

Introduction

There is an old saying: "You are what you eat." It could not be more true. The foods you eat, and the liquids you drink, go towards making up your body – your skin and bones, muscles and nerves, heart and blood and all other parts. When you eat foods, your body changes them into **nutrients**, which are like microscopic "building blocks" for your body. The nutrients become incorporated into your body's structure. It is a complex process involving many physical and chemical changes.

When you are young and growing, the body is making new and bigger parts all the time. Also, as you absorb and use "new" nutrients, "old" nutrients (in an "old" part of the body) are dismantled and removed as wastes. There is a constant turnover of growth and repair, as old, damaged and worn-out parts are disposed of, and new ones are built to take their place. This is why you have to keep eating, day after day.

Foods provide not only the body's building materials, they also provide energy. For things to happen, energy is required. Running, jumping, swimming and writing all use energy. So do reading, thinking and daydreaming. The human body is using energy all the time, even when asleep. It must keep itself warm, pump blood around, repair damaged parts, absorb foods and get rid of wastes. All these activities need energy.

The nutrients and energy in foods are broken down into the substances the body needs. This process is called digestion.

What we eat

- The average adult eats about 500 kg (1,100 lb) of foods in a year.
- In a typical day, the body takes in about 450 g (16 oz) of **carbohydrates** and **fats** (page 8) for energy, and 60 g (2 oz) of **protein** for "building-block" nutrients.
- It also takes in half a gram (about 1/50 oz) of the **mineral** calcium (page 10), for healthy bones and teeth, and 10 milligrams (1/100th of a gram) of iron, mainly for healthy blood.

▽ Food comes in many forms, from these fresh vegetables to peanuts to barbecued steaks.

4

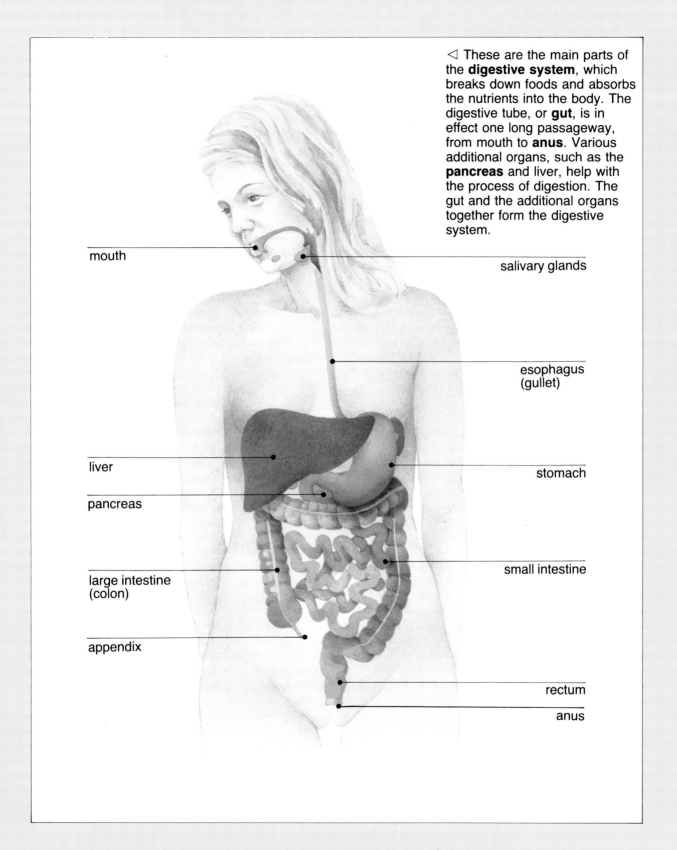

◁ These are the main parts of the **digestive system**, which breaks down foods and absorbs the nutrients into the body. The digestive tube, or **gut**, is in effect one long passageway, from mouth to **anus**. Various additional organs, such as the **pancreas** and liver, help with the process of digestion. The gut and the additional organs together form the digestive system.

mouth

salivary glands

esophagus (gullet)

liver

stomach

pancreas

large intestine (colon)

small intestine

appendix

rectum

anus

Our daily diet

Measuring energy in food

- Energy in food is often measured in units called calories. Calories represent the energy-producing value in food when oxidized in the body. Energy is also measured in joules, and 1 calorie equals 4.19 joules.
- For example, a lettuce leaf contains about 5 calories, a slice of bread about 80, and a helping of cheesecake or a hamburger about 400.
- The amount of energy a person needs each day depends largely on how active he or she is.
- A person with a fairly active job, such as a construction worker, needs around 3,000-3,500 calories each day.
- Someone with a less active job, such as a desk clerk, might need about 2,000-2,500 calories each day.
- A pregnant mother needs up to 800 calories extra each day, for her growing baby.
- If you take in more calories than you need, they will be changed into fat tissue.

The foods and drinks we take in each day are called our diet. (The word "diet" is sometimes used to mean eating less food in order to lose weight, as when someone "goes on a diet.")

Diets differ enormously. They vary according to where we live, from one country to another, and even between the city and the countryside. They vary with family background, the types of foods available locally (in the stores or homegrown), and which foods are in season. Diets are also affected by how much money we spend on food, how much we like cooking, and of course our own personal likes and dislikes – our "taste" in food. They also vary according to what the experts – nutritionists and dieticians – say is good or bad.

However much they vary, all diets can be described in terms of six main types of substance. These are proteins, carbohydrates, fats, **vitamins**, minerals and **fiber**. Any food, from a potato to a walnut to a sausage, can be analysed to see how much of each of these it contains. The body needs each of the six types in different amounts, and for different reasons, as explained on the next few pages.

A seventh part of the diet provides no nutrients or energy, but it is vital for our survival. It is water, which is essential for all life. Water is present in every food, and especially in drinks. Most healthy people could survive for many days without eating. But the body could not last more than a few days, at most, without water.

△ For humans, a meal is not just a time to take in more food, to fuel the body. We enjoy the colors, textures and flavors of the dishes. A meal is also a social time, when we discuss family matters and the events of the day.

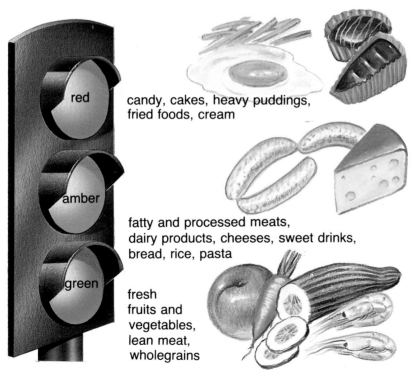

red — candy, cakes, heavy puddings, fried foods, cream

amber — fatty and processed meats, dairy products, cheeses, sweet drinks, bread, rice, pasta

green — fresh fruits and vegetables, lean meat, wholegrains

◁ The "traffic-light guide," devised by England's Health Education Authority, is one way to avoid becoming overweight by eating healthily. For red-light foods, stop and think. For amber-light foods, go carefully. For green-light foods, go right ahead. Here are some examples of the foods in each category.

Proteins, carbohydrates, fats

△ Many "power" athletes like weightlifters and shot-putters eat big, high-protein meals as part of their training. This provides lots of energy and raw materials for muscle building.

Very few foods contain only protein, or just carbohydrates, or nothing but fat. Most foods are a mixture of the six main types of substance. However, certain foods tend to contain a lot of one or two types of substance, and less of the others. We can put foods into "groups," in order to plan a healthy diet and benefit the body.

Proteins are the main raw materials for growth, repair and replacement. Foods that are rich in proteins include meat, fish, eggs, cheese, beans, dried peas and similar vegetables, and also grains and breads, to a lesser extent. These "body-

▷ Energy for the marathon: these runners have more than 26 miles to cover. Energy is stored in many forms in their bodies, including blood sugar, body starch in the muscles and liver, and fatty tissue.

building" foods are the main source of building-block nutrients, although they can be converted into energy if required. They also give taste and texture to a meal.

Carbohydrates are the body's main energy source. Foods that contain plenty of **starchy** carbohydrates include potatoes, pastas, cereals, bread, rice, and also some fruits and nuts. They contain plenty of quickly-available calories, for powering the chemical reactions that keep the body alive and active.

Fats are contained in foods such as milk, butter, cheese and other dairy products, meats, and also in certain plant substances such as olives, peanuts, sunflower seeds and soy beans. There are several types of fats. In general it is healthier to take in plant fats rather than animal fats – although too much of any fat can be bad for the body. Fats are rich in energy and they are also needed in small amounts by the body, for growth and repair. They tend to make a meal more "filling" and "tasty."

The body does not need all these dietary substances in equal amounts. Indeed, this would be harmful. For example, too much of some types of fats increases the risk of heart disease. In terms of energy, a healthy diet should provide about half its energy in the form of carbohydrates, a third or less as fats, and the rest as proteins. This is one aspect of what we call a healthy **balanced diet**.

Diet changes through life. Babies and children need plenty of proteins, for making new body tissues, and also lots of carbohydrates for energy since they tend to be very active. Later in life, some people become less active and so do not need to eat as much food.

Fats and heart disease

- Many medical studies around the world have shown there is a link between too much fat in the diet and heart disease.
- In the United States heart disease is the number one cause of death. In Britain, it kills about one-third of all people who die in middle and old age.
- Eating less fatty foods, especially the animal fats contained in dairy products and red meats, helps to reduce the risk of heart disease.
- Even children can start to develop the underlying cause of heart disease. So it is never too soon to start eating sensibly.

Vitamins, minerals and fiber

◁ "Fresh is best." Fresh fruits, like these, and fresh vegetables are particularly rich in vitamins and are very good for the body. Cooking tends to destroy such vitamins, and prolonged boiling dissolves them out into the water.

The other three main types of substance are vitamins, minerals and fiber. They contain no energy, but are essential for a balanced diet.

Vitamins are chemicals which the body needs for growth, repair and other vital functions, but only in very small amounts. A few vitamins can be assembled in the body from substances in the diet, but most have to be taken in ready-made, from a wide variety of foods. Each vitamin has a letter and a chemical name. For instance, vitamin C is also known as ascorbic acid, and is found especially in fresh vegetables, oranges, lemons, blackcurrants and other fruits.

Minerals are substances such as calcium, iron, phosphorus, potassium and magnesium. Some are used in various body processes. For example, sodium and potassium are required for nerve signals to pass along nerves, while phosphorus is involved in the process of releasing energy from foods. Other minerals are incorporated into the body's tissues, such as calcium, which helps to build bones and teeth. There is a long list of minerals needed by the body but, like vitamins, most are required only in small amounts.

Fiber, or "roughage," comes from plants. It is contained in wholegrains, bread (especially wholemeal), cereals, legumes such as lentils, and other vegetables and fruits. The body cannot digest or absorb it. But plenty of fiber gives "bulk" to food, helps the digestive system to work well, and reduces the risks of diseases.

▽ The foods shown below are rich in certain vitamins, which the body needs for a range of functions. Vitamin A is needed for growth and resistance to infection, and for maintaining healthy skin and eyes. Vitamin K is essential for blood clotting, to stop bleeding from wounds. Lack of a vitamin can cause what is known as a vitamin deficiency disease. One example is scurvy, caused by lack of vitamin C.

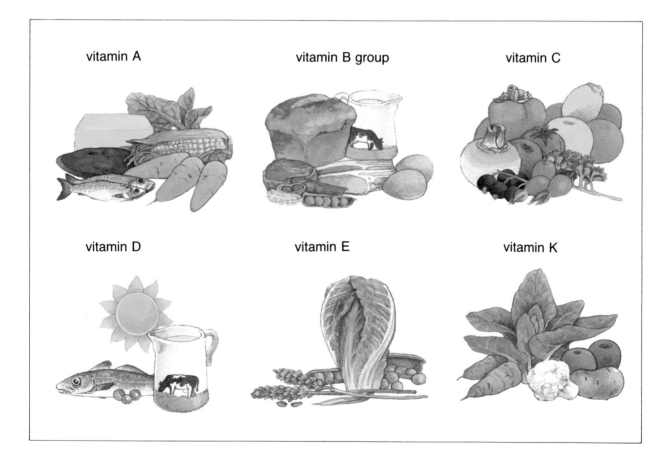

vitamin A

vitamin B group

vitamin C

vitamin D

vitamin E

vitamin K

The chemistry of digestion

Before foods can be absorbed into the body, they have to be broken down into tiny pieces called molecules. The various molecules must be small enough to dissolve in water so that they can pass through the wall of the digestive tube into the body. This process happens gradually as food travels from the mouth down into the stomach, and then along the tube-like **intestines**.

Glands along the length of the digestive system produce strong chemicals such as acids, **alkalis** and **enzymes**. These attack the foods chemically, breaking them into smaller and smaller pieces. There are several kinds of enzymes, and each one breaks down a certain kind of food. **Pepsin** and **trypsin** attack protein foods such as meats, while **amylase** and maltase work on carbohydrate foods. Fats do not dissolve in water, instead forming blob-like drops. They are first broken down into tiny droplets (emulsified) and then worked on by enzymes called lipases.

Some enzymes work in acidic conditions, while others need alkaline surroundings. As foods move through each region of the digestive system, they are flooded with mixtures of acid and enzymes, or alkali and enzymes. These corrosive liquids gradually break down the food substances.

The meat we eat is made of the same kinds of materials as our own digestive system. So why do the meat-attacking enzymes not digest our own gut? The inner lining of the gut produces a coat of thick, sticky **mucus** for protection.

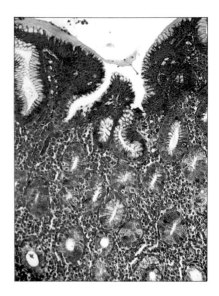

△ The light microscope (at about 70 times magnification) shows a cross-section of the stomach wall, with the circular and tube-like gastric pits. The blue cells line the pit walls. Cells around the bottom of each pit make digestive juices such as **hydrochloric acid**.

12

▽ Digestion is a complicated process. As the foods pass along the digestive system, they are broken down in a series of steps. This diagrammatic view of the digestive system shows the different parts and how they link together, with nutrients as colored dots.

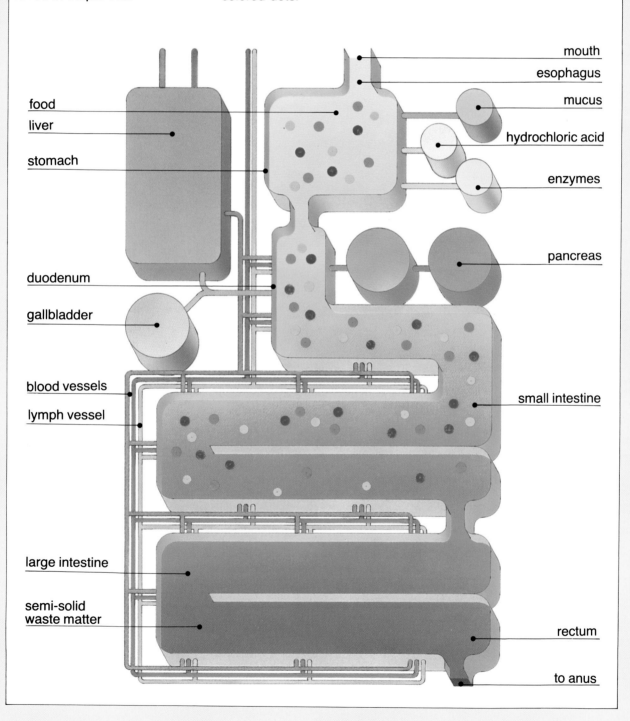

mouth

esophagus

mucus

food

liver

hydrochloric acid

stomach

enzymes

pancreas

duodenum

gallbladder

blood vessels

small intestine

lymph vessel

large intestine

semi-solid waste matter

rectum

to anus

The gut, a digestive tube

The gut, or "digestive tube," starts at the mouth and finishes at the anus. It is about eight meters (26 ft) long in an adult.

A typical part of the gut, such as the intestine, is made up of several layers. The inner lining is called the **mucosa** and may be wrinkled or folded, to give a large surface area for production of digestive chemicals and absorption of nutrients. This layer contains many microscopic glands which pour out, or secrete, the many digestive chemicals such as enzymes, acid and alkali. The mucosa is coated on the inside with mucus, which protects it from the chemicals and also from any germs that might be in the foods.

▽ The gut is built on the basic plan shown below. Each layer has a specific function. In some regions of the gut, a layer may be much thicker or thinner, depending on its job in that region.

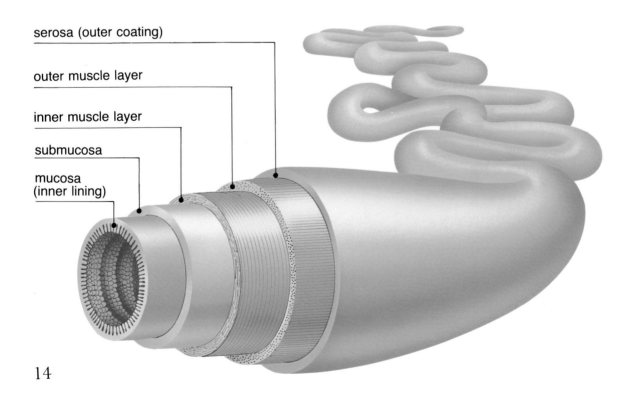

serosa (outer coating)

outer muscle layer

inner muscle layer

submucosa

mucosa
(inner lining)

14

Around the mucosa is the **submucosa**, which is tough and elastic and forms a strong "framework" for the gut. It contains blood vessels that nourish the other layers, and nerves that control the muscles of the gut.

The gut muscles are wrapped around the submucosa and form the next two layers. They act to push food through the inside of the gut, by the process known as **peristalsis** (page 16).

The outer coating of the gut is known as the serosa. It protects the gut and lubricates it, so that it can slip and slide easily, as the muscles of the gut contract and make it squirm about inside the body.

This basic plan of the gut changes from one region to the next, along its length. For example, the stomach is a much-enlarged bulbous portion, which acts as a "reservoir" and swells enormously to hold a large meal. The small intestine, on the other hand, is much longer but very narrow.

▽ A doctor may look at the inside of gut through an endoscope. This flexible, telescope-like device can be passed into the patient's mouth and down into the stomach or intestine. This view shows the folds of the stomach lining. The image is conveyed along the endoscope by dozens of optical fibers, which produce the tiny mosaic-like effect.

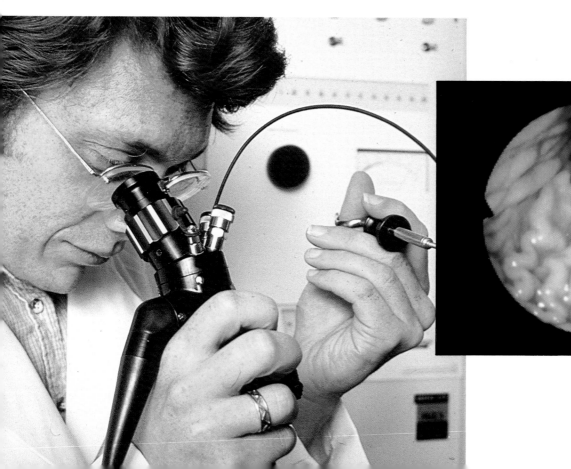

Squeezing and pushing

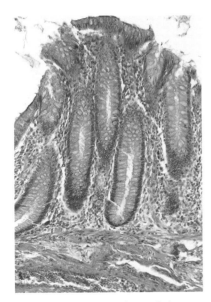

△ A microscopic view of the gut wall, with the inner muscle layer at the bottom.

The gut is long and folded. Most of it is tightly packed into the abdomen, and internal body pressure squashes it flat. Therefore foods cannot pass through it unaided – they must be pushed. The process of peristalsis moves the food along. Its journey is lubricated by the slippery mucus that lines the inside of the gut.

Peristalsis is carried out by the two layers of muscles in the gut wall. The fibers of the inner muscle layer are wrapped around the gut, like many short elastic bands encircling the tube. The fibers of the outer muscle layer stretch lengthwise, running along its length.

Peristalsis is a muscular action that involves both muscle layers working in a coordinated fashion. Two nerve networks control the muscles.

Ring of muscle contracts behind food

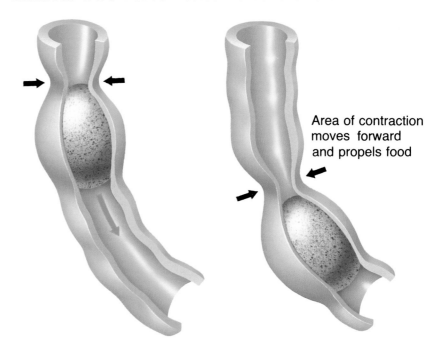

Area of contraction moves forward and propels food

▷ In peristalsis, a "wave of contraction" moves along the gut. This pushes a lump of food in front of it, and so keeps the contents moving.

16

These are the myenteric plexus, between the muscle layers, and the submucosal plexus, in the submucosa on the inside of the muscle layers.

First, the inner muscle layer just behind the food contracts. This makes the gut narrower at this point and pushes the food forward a little. The food has been mashed up and partly liquified in the mouth, so it oozes along easily. Next, the outer muscle layer contracts to shorten the length of that part of the gut. At the same time the narrowed portion moves along the gut, pushing the food in front of it.

This muscular action moves along the gut like a wave, pushing the food. There are many peristaltic waves, one after the other, which gradually squeeze and "massage" the food along. In the esophagus, the waves travel towards the stomach at about 3 to 5 centimeters (1 to 2 ins) per second. Normally you are upright when you eat, so gravity helps the waves to propel swallowed food down to the stomach. However, the peristaltic waves in the esophagus are so strong that they can push food against gravity.

In some regions of the gut, at the appropriate time, the peristaltic waves slow down or stop. This allows food to remain in that region while thorough digestion takes place. Then the waves speed up and become stronger again.

If the gut is irritated by an infection or harmful substances in the food, the muscles and the nerve networks may not work correctly. Peristalsis may be too rapid for proper digestion to take place, so that the wastes at the other end are loose and watery. This is one cause of diarrhea. Or peristalsis might be too slow or weak, and the wastes move too slowly. This is a cause of constipation.

How fast does food travel?

- A meal takes anything from 12 to 36 hours to pass through the gut, from the mouth to the other end.
- The time taken depends mainly on the size of the meal, and the amount of fiber it contains.
- As you swallow, it takes only a few seconds for foods to pass down the esophagus.
- A big meal may stay in the stomach for 5 hours or more.
- About 5 to 10 hours after eating, the food is passing along the intestines.
- Some 10 to 15 hours after the meal, semi-solid wastes (**feces**) are forming near the end of the gut.

First stop for food: the mouth

Some foods are minced, sliced, cut up and cooked before we eat them. Others can be eaten raw. Some are hard, like nuts, and others are soft and squishy. The mouth deals with all these different kinds and sizes of foods. It is the first region of the gut, and begins the physical and chemical processes of digestion.

Some foods are very dry and scratchy. As we chew, a watery fluid called saliva produced in glands around the mouth, is mixed into the food. It helps to soften, moisten and lubricate the food, ready for swallowing. It also contains an enzyme (amylase) that even at this first stage begins the chemical attack on carbohydrates.

Teeth do the biting and chewing. They cut and

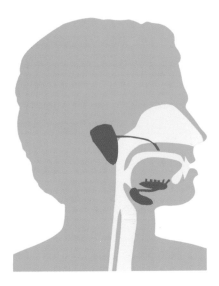

△ Saliva is produced in three pairs of salivary glands, shown in red. About 1.5 liters or quarts are made daily.

◁ Brushing teeth two or three times daily helps to keep them clean and healthy. Brush for at least three minutes, using mainly up-and-down and small circular strokes.

18

mash foods into pulpy lumps which can be easily swallowed. Each tooth is covered by a white layer of enamel, the hardest substance in the body.

There are four types of teeth, each adapted to a certain job. The front eight teeth (two on each side, in both upper and lower jaws) are called incisors. They are shaped like chisels to bite and slice off chunks of food. Next to these are four long canines, for tearing food into large lumps. Behind these are eight premolars, which mash and squash the food. At the back of the mouth are the 12 molars, which grind and chew. This makes a total of 32 teeth for an adult.

Babies grow a total of 20 "milk" (or deciduous) teeth, in the first few years of life. These fall out and are gradually replaced by permanent teeth.

Other parts of the mouth are also involved. The tongue pushes foods about so that we can cut and chew them thoroughly. Taste buds on the tongue tell us if a food has a good flavor, and whether it is "bad" and possibly poisonous.

A healthy mouth

If bits of food are left in the mouth, they can rot and cause health problems. Keeping teeth, gums and mouth clean is called oral hygiene.

- Keep the teeth and gums clean by brushing after each meal, and before going to bed.
- Brush all parts of the teeth, both front and back and in between, to get rid of stale food.
- Use fluoride toothpaste. Fluoride is a mineral that helps to strengthen enamel.
- Eat sugary and sweet foods less often.
- Go to the dentist regularly, so that any bad teeth or gum problems can be detected and dealt with at an early stage.

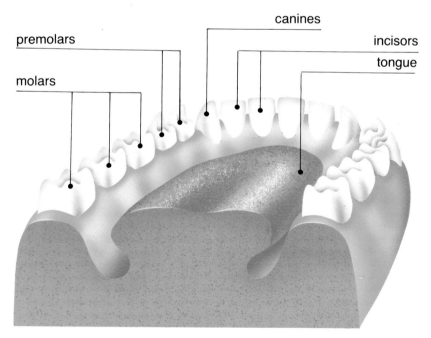

premolars

molars

canines

incisors

tongue

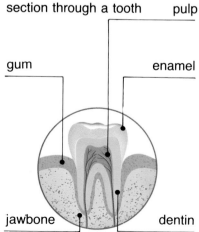

◁ Teeth are set firmly into the jawbone, and each is shaped for a certain job.

section through a tooth   pulp

gum   enamel

jawbone   dentin

19

Second stage: the esophagus

△ Even in space, where there is no gravity, astronauts can swallow their meals easily. Peristalsis in the esophagus pushes the food down into the stomach.

The esophagus, or gullet, is the second main region of the gut. It is a muscular tube about 25 centimeters (10 in) long, just behind the trachea (windpipe), connecting the throat to the stomach.

As you swallow, the tongue pushes a lump of food towards the back of the mouth and into the top portion of the throat, which is called the pharynx. As this happens, the top of the trachea rises upward and a small flap, the epiglottis, folds over to cover its entrance. This prevents the food from "going down the wrong way" and entering the trachea instead of the esophagus, which could cause choking.

Muscular waves of peristalsis push the lump of food, known as a bolus, down the esophagus and into the stomach. At the base of the esophagus there is a valve-like arrangement of muscle called the esophageal **sphincter**, which is normally tightly closed. As food arrives from above, the valve relaxes and allows it to pass through into the stomach; it quickly closes again afterwards, to seal off the passageway. This system stops the stomach contents, which are strongly acidic, from welling up into the bottom of the esophagus.

Sometimes the esophageal sphincter does not work properly. This may be because of obesity (being overweight), or if you bend forwards and down when the stomach is very full. The stomach's acidic contents push up into the lower part of the esophagus and cause a sharp burning feeling we call "heartburn."

▷ In the medical test known as a barium swallow, the person drinks a cupful of a substance called barium sulphate. This shows up white on the X-ray screen and outlines the esophagus as it travels down to the stomach. Here the neck bones are the shadowy white bones at the top left, and the shapes of the ribs can be seen to the right. The barium is the bright white mass in the center.

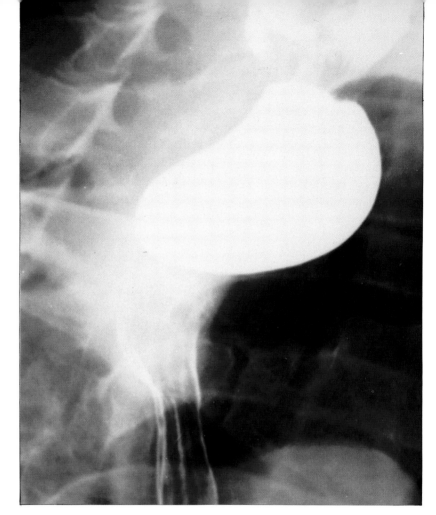

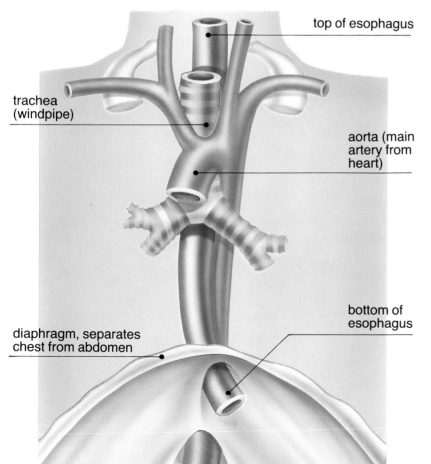

top of esophagus

trachea (windpipe)

aorta (main artery from heart)

diaphragm, separates chest from abdomen

bottom of esophagus

◁ The esophagus passes through the chest, squeezing between the lungs and their airways, and the heart and its main blood vesels. Food must be actively pushed along to force it past all these parts and into the abdomen.

21

Stage three: the stomach

The stomach is a very tough, muscular, J-shaped bag. When almost empty, it has a volume of about half a liter (2 cups). It can easily expand to hold an average meal plus drink, with a volume of one and a half liters or quarts. It can stretch to twice this size for a large meal. The muscles in the stomach will contract strongly in peristaltic waves to churn and squash foods that have already been chewed in the mouth.

The esophagus joins the stomach near its broad upper part, called the **fundus**. The lower part, the **pylorus**, does most of the churning and this is where the main digestive processes occur.

▽ On the outside, the stomach has bands of muscles wrapped around its lining. Inside, the lining is folded into pits and ridges.

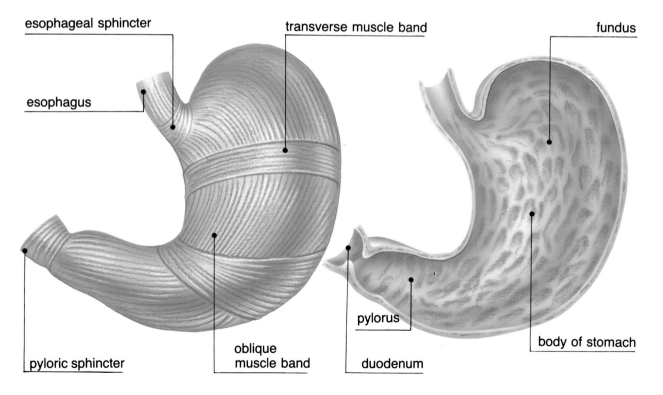

esophageal sphincter

esophagus

transverse muscle band

fundus

pyloric sphincter

oblique muscle band

pylorus

duodenum

body of stomach

22

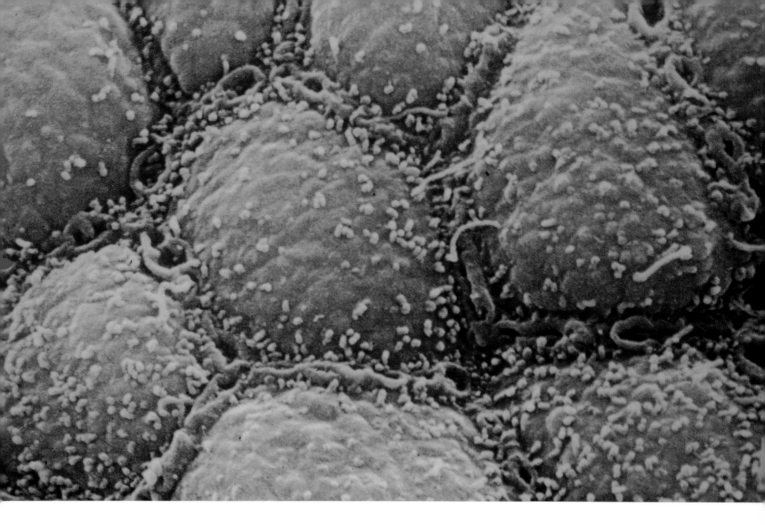

The stomach usually contains a small amount of gas, as a result of swallowing air with food. The presence of this gas allows the liquified food to slop about as it is mixed and squeezed by peristalsis, causing "stomach rumbling."

The stomach lining contains millions of tiny glands. These make a digestive liquid called gastric juice, which contains the chemical hydrochloric acid. The acid attacks the food and softens it, as part of the process of chemical digestion. The acid also destroys germs in food, helping to protect the gut from infection.

Glands in the stomach lining also make an enzyme-like substance, **pepsinogen**. When this meets the stomach acid it is converted into the enzyme pepsin, which begins to digest the proteins in the food.

△ Under the scanning electron microscope, the folds of the stomach's inner surface look like rows of cobblestones. Thick mucus (slime) shields the lining from digestion by stomach juices. Most of the mucus has been removed in order to make this photograph, but small flecks of it are still scattered about like raindrops.

The duodenum, the fourth stage

The soupy, sloppy food which leaves the stomach is called **chyme**. Small amounts of chyme are squirted regularly from the stomach through another valve-like ring of muscle, the pyloric (or duodenal) sphincter, and into the first part of the small intestine. This is known as the **duodenum**. It is some 25 centimeters (10 in) long and bent into a horseshoe shape around the broad end of the pancreas, one of the digestive system's glands.

The chyme that enters the duodenum is strongly acidic, and it would corrode the intestines further on. So it is neutralized by alkali in the duodenum. This also stops the action of the enzyme pepsin, which only works in acidic

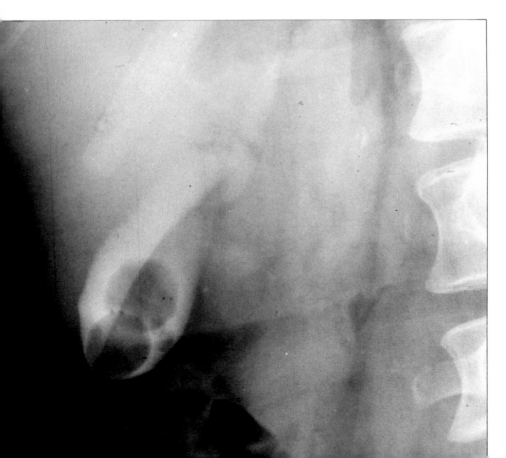

◁ In the medical photograph known as a cholecystogram, dye which shows up white on X-ray is swallowed and concentrates in the liver and gall bladder. This patient's gall bladder (the long, pear-shaped bag, lower left) contains two dark, rounded shadows which are gallstones.

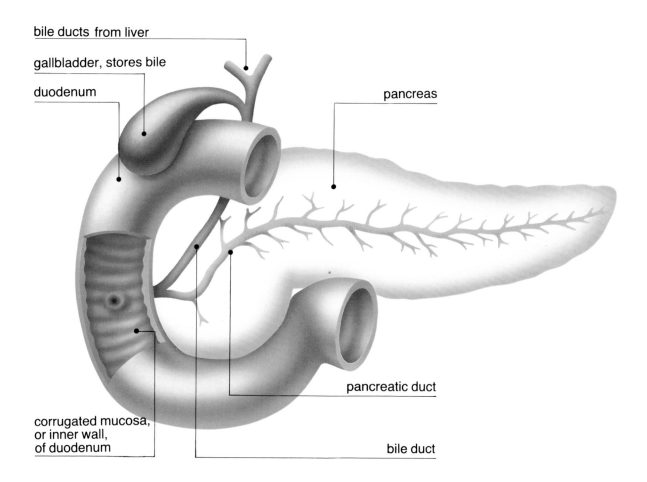

bile ducts from liver

gallbladder, stores bile

duodenum

pancreas

pancreatic duct

corrugated mucosa,
or inner wall,
of duodenum

bile duct

conditions. However, other enzymes which function well in the now-alkaline surroundings take over digestion.

Two small tubes come together and join the duodenum about 10 centimeters (4 in) along its length. These tubes carry digestive fluids from the pancreas and the gall bladder. The gall bladder is a small muscular bag about 8 centimeters (3 in) long and can hold up to 50 milliliters (1.6 fl oz) of the greenish-yellow liquid known as **bile**.

Bile is made in the liver and stored in the gall bladder. When chyme from a meal starts to flow through the duodenum, the gall bladder contracts and squirts bile along the bile duct into the duodenum. Bile contains emulsifying chemicals which help to break up blobs of fats in the chyme.

△ The duodenum curves around the broad end of the pancreas. Two small tubes, the pancreatic duct and the bile duct, come together and empty their digestive fluids through a small hole into the duodenum.

The pancreas

The pancreas nestles in the upper left abdomen, behind the stomach, around the level of the lower ribs. It is shaped like a thin triangle about 15 centimeters (6 in) in length, with its broad "head" towards the center of the body, and a tapering "tail" on the left side, in front of the left kidney.

The pancreas is a dual-function gland. One of its jobs is to make an enzyme-containing juice for digestion. The other is to make a **hormone** (body chemical) called **insulin**.

The pancreas produces the pancreatic juice, which contains many strong enzymes that carry out digestion in the duodenum and small intestine. The juice is collected by a network of small tubes that join to form the main pancreatic

▽ This photograph through a light microscope reveals one of the islets of Langerhans in the pancreas. The islet shows as a rounded group of lighter-colored cells in the center. The islet is surrounded by cells which make digestive juice.

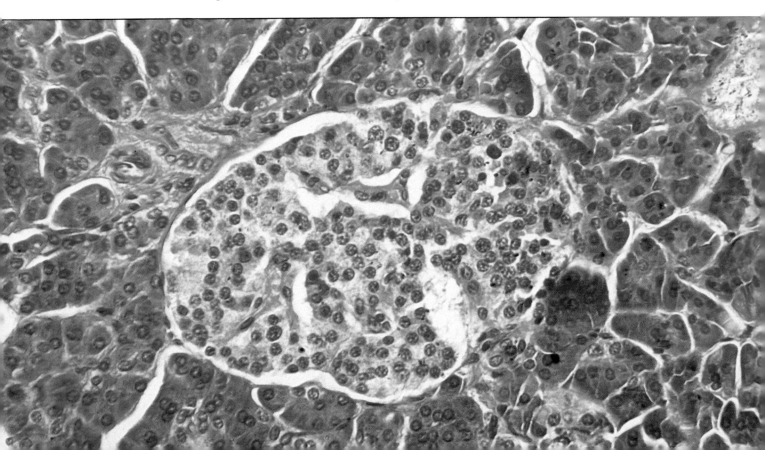

duct, which connects to the duodenum.

These enzymes are too powerful to be made in their active form inside the pancreas – otherwise they would digest the pancreatic tissue itself. Like pepsin in the stomach, the pancreatic enzymes are manufactured in inactive form. They are then converted into the active enzymes by the alkaline conditions in the duodenum.

The second function of the pancreas is to make insulin, a body chemical which is part of the hormonal system. Insulin helps to control the amount of sugar in the bloodstream and the way cells use energy. It is released straight into the blood, flowing through the pancreas rather than being channeled along ducts like the digestive pancreatic juice. The pancreatic cells that make insulin are scattered throughout the gland, in small groups called the islets of Langerhans. There are about one million islets in a normal pancreas, but they make up less than one-hundredth of the weight of this gland.

Pancreatic juice

The juice made by the pancreas contains various enzymes and other chemicals for digestion.
● Trypsin and **chymotrypsin** continue the attack on proteins, begun in the stomach by pepsin.
● Amylase works to break up carbohydrates into smaller molecules.
● Lipase helps to digest the fats which have been emulsified by bile.
● The pancreatic juice also contains alkali, which neutralizes the acidic chyme in the duodenum.

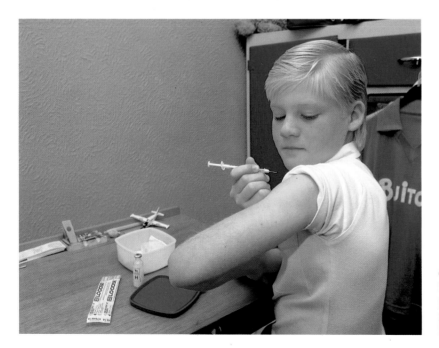

◁ The condition known as diabetes is due to a lack of insulin production by the pancreas. Some diabetic people replace the missing insulin daily by injection.

27

Small intestine, stage five

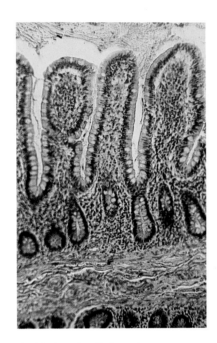

△ Under the light microscope, the villi lining the small intestine look like rows of fingers. Enterocytes, the cells that cover each villus, live for about four days before they are rubbed off by the intestinal contents passing by.

So far along the gut there has been much digestion of foods, but little absorption of the resulting nutrients into the body. The stomach takes in certain substances, such as alcohol and some sugars. But most absorption takes place in the rest of the small intestine, directly after the duodenum.

The small intestine is actually very long, around 4 to 6 meters (13–17 ft). It is called "small" because it is so narrow, with a diameter of only 3 to 4 centimeters (1–1.5 in). It is tightly looped and coiled in the central part of the abdomen.

The inner lining of the small intestine has an enormous surface area, in order to absorb as many nutrients as efficiently as possible. This great area is made possible by three features. First, the lining is ridged and folded, rather than being smooth. Second, the ridges are covered in millions of tiny finger-like projections called **villi**, which give it a fluffy, velvety nature. Third, the villi bear their own microscopic finger-like structures, known as **microvilli**.

The small intestine's lining has a rich blood supply. The nutrients from digestion are by now in the form of small molecules such as **amino acids** (from proteins), **sugars** (from carbohydrates) and triglycerides (from fats). These can pass through the lining cells and into the blood vessels beneath. Triglycerides tend to pass into lacteals, which are part of the body's "alternative" circulation, the lymphatic system.

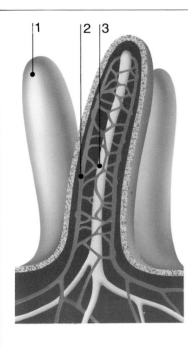

1 2 3

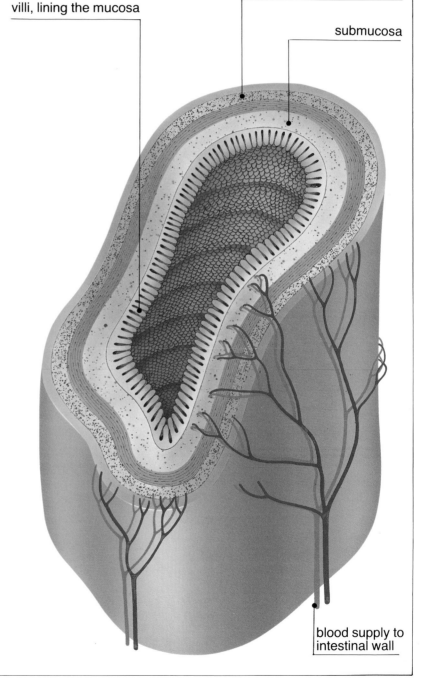

△ The villi in the small intestine (1) have a network of blood **capillaries** and **lymph** vessels inside them. Fresh blood nourishes the intestinal wall; as it flows away (2), it carries dissolved nutrients for processing by the liver and other organs. Fats pass into the lacteals (3) and eventually find their way into the blood, too.

▽ A cut-through view of the small intestine shows the various layers in its wall, and the ridges and villi of the lining.

villi, lining the mucosa

muscle layers

submucosa

blood supply to intestinal wall

Stage six: the large intestine

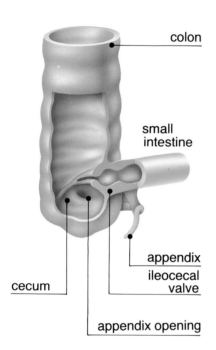

colon

small intestine

appendix

ileocecal valve

cecum

appendix opening

△ At the junction of the small and large intestines, there is a little structure about the size and shape of a finger, known as the **appendix**. It seems to have no useful function, and is thought to be an "evolutionary left-over" from our distant ancestors.

The end of the small intestine marks the end of digestion, but not of absorption. By now the intestinal contents are made of various indigestible materials – and water. However, this water and the dissolved mineral salts it carries are valuable for the body. In order to prevent their loss (which would mean we would have to drink lots more liquid), water is absorbed in the last part of the gut, the large intestine.

The large intestine (also called the large bowel) is about 1.5 to 2 meters (5 to 6 ft) long and has three main parts. The first is short and wide, and is known as the cecum. Watery, unabsorbed materials flow into the cecum from the small intestine, under control of a sphincter-like structure, the ileocecal valve.

Next the materials pass into the **colon**, a wide tube about 6 to 7 centimeters (2 to 3 in) in diameter. The colon is shaped like an upside-down U and goes up the right side of the abdomen, across the top and down the left side. Here the valuable water and salts are absorbed through the lining into the body. As this happens, the materials become less fluid and change into the brownish, moist, semi-solid feces or stools.

The third part of the large intestine is the **rectum**. It is about 12 centimeters (5 in) long and can stretch to store some of the feces as they are passed to the outside (defecated). This happens through the final part of the gut, the anus, which is another muscular sphincter.

What makes up the wastes?

The digestive wastes known as feces are made up of various substances.

- Water makes up about three-fifths of the weight of feces.
- Without the water, about one-third of the dry weight is undigested parts of food, such as fiber, that have passed straight through the gut.
- Another third is dead bacteria. In a healthy person, millions of "friendly" bacteria live in the intestines and help in the digestive and absorptive processes.
- The final third consists of unwanted mineral salts, mucus, bile contents and rubbed-off bits of gut lining.
- The rectum, the final part of the large intestine, is usually empty. It fills with feces a short time before defecation, when the anal muscles relax and allow abdominal pressure to squeeze the wastes through.

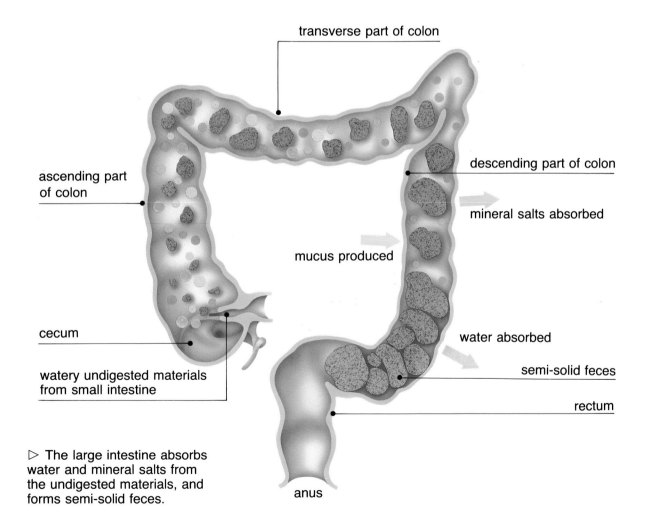

transverse part of colon

ascending part of colon

descending part of colon

mineral salts absorbed

mucus produced

cecum

water absorbed

watery undigested materials from small intestine

semi-solid feces

rectum

anus

▷ The large intestine absorbs water and mineral salts from the undigested materials, and forms semi-solid feces.

Control of the digestive system

Digestion is a long and complicated process, and it needs careful control. It would be wasteful for the stomach to secrete acid if there was no food inside it, or for the pancreas to release its juices after the foods had passed through the duodenum In fact, such illtiming can actually be harmful (page 34).

Like many other body processes, digestion is under dual control. The nervous system and hormonal system work together to ensure that foods are moved through the gut at the right speed, and that the digestive juices are prepared and ready to be added to the foods on arrival.

The sight, smell, taste or even the thought of food puts the digestive system into action. We may imagine a favorite meal – and at once saliva starts to flow from the salivary glands into the mouth, ready to moisten and lubricate the food, even though it is not there yet. This is why we say a meal is "mouth-watering."

Most nervous control of digestion happens automatically, without us being aware of it. For example, the cells in the stomach that make gastric juices are controlled by the vagus nerve, which runs down from the brain stem (the lower part of the brain). The smell and taste of food, and its presence in the mouth, esophagus and stomach are detected, and nerve signals are sent to the brain. The brain sends out signals along the vagus nerve to the stomach lining, where the cells produce and release their juices. The stomach

The fluids of digestion

During digestion, many watery fluids are made by the body while others are absorbed. It is an intricate example of recycling water several times, so that we do not have to drink too much.

- The salivary glands produce 1.5 to 2 liters or quarts of saliva each day.
- The stomach manufactures 1.5 to 2 liters or quarts of gastric juice daily.
- The liver makes around 1 liter or quart of bile per day, which is stored and concentrated in the gall bladder.
- The pancreas makes 1 to 1.5 liters or quarts of pancreatic juice daily.
- In total, about 10 to 12 liters (2 to 3 gallons) of watery contents flow through the gut every day. But less than 0.1 liter or quart is lost in the feces.

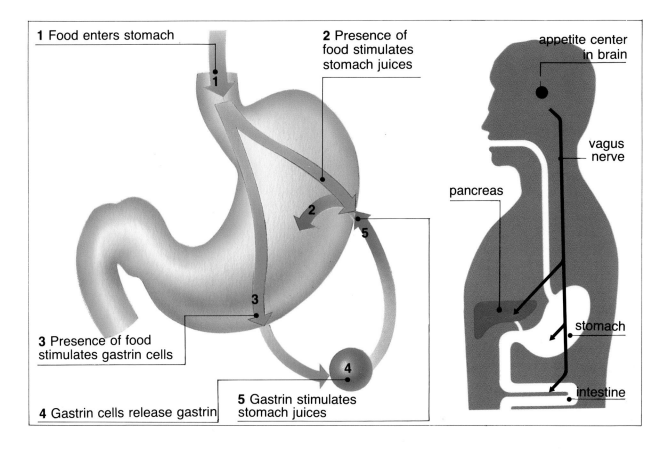

1 Food enters stomach

2 Presence of food stimulates stomach juices

3 Presence of food stimulates gastrin cells

4 Gastrin cells release gastrin

5 Gastrin stimulates stomach juices

appetite center in brain

vagus nerve

pancreas

stomach

intestine

△ Nerves and hormones work together to control digestion. Food entering the stomach causes production of gastrin, which stimulates the juice-making cells in the lining (left). The vagus nerve brings nerve messages from the brain to the stomach and other organs (right).

also begins its writhing peristaltic movements. This extra activity is the cause of the stomach "rumbling" when we are hungry.

Hormones, the body's "chemical messengers," are also involved. The nerve signals from the vagus act on special cells in the lining of the upper part of the stomach. These cells make the hormone gastrin, which passes into the local blood supply around the stomach. When gastrin reaches the stomach's juice-making cells, it stimulates them into activity too.

The control systems also work to slow down processes. As the duodenum fills with a batch of chyme from the stomach, sensors in its wall detect the stretching. They send nerve signals back to the stomach, which moderate its churning movements and so slow the flow of chyme.

Digestive system disorders

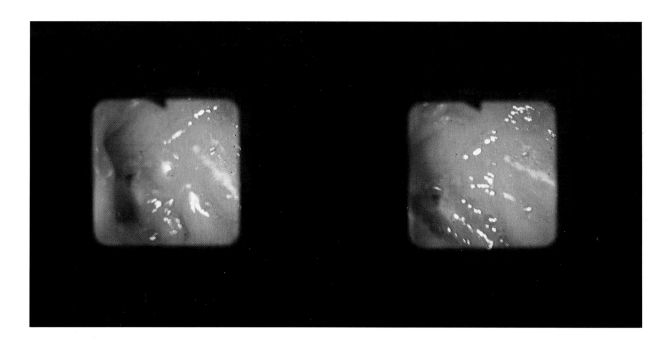

As digestion is a complicated process, it is not surprising that things go wrong occasionally. We may harm the body by eating too much or too little food, or by eating unwisely.

Sometimes we eat bad food, or there is too much and the digestive system cannot cope. In certain cases, the body reacts by vomiting (bringing up) the stomach contents. This is done by peristaltic contractions moving in the reverse direction, squeezing the stomach and then traveling up the esophagus. Contraction of the general abdominal muscles also helps to push the stomach contents upward and out.

The strong, corrosive fluids which digest food can cause problems. The protective mucous

△ Through an endoscope, the doctor can examine the stomach and duodenal linings and search for ulcers, cuts and worn areas (abrasions and erosions).

coating inside the stomach or duodenum may fail, for various reasons. For example, the stomach may make too much acid, and release it when there are no foods inside to soak it up. The acid erodes a raw spot in the lining, which becomes sore and painful. This is an ulcer. Another name for a stomach ulcer is gastric ulcer; a "peptic" ulcer is either a stomach or duodenal ulcer.

Occasionally, the appendix becomes blocked for some reason and traps gut contents in the dead-end space inside it. As the contents begin to decay, they irritate the appendix and make it swollen and sore, and possibly infected. This disorder, known as appendicitis, can be extremely painful. An emergency operation may be needed.

△ In many parts of the world digestive problems, such as infection, mean the body loses too much fluid and body salts, as diarrhea or vomit (page 37). These people are learning how to replace the fluid by oral rehydration therapy, and so help sufferers to recover.

Gut infections and hygiene

Basic food hygiene

Cut down the chance of gut infections by following simple guidelines. For example:
- Always wash hands before touching food or cooking utensils.
- Also, wash hands after using the lavatory.
- Keep the cooking area very clean, and make sure wastebaskets are covered and not near the foods.
- Be sure cooking and eating utensils have been properly washed, rinsed and dried.
- Store foods in clean containers. Keep them in the refrigerator, as necessary.
- Do not leave warm foods uncovered, since germs can land on them and breed.
- Cook food thoroughly, according to the instructions in a good cookbook.
- Check the "sell by" dates on foods bought from stores.

Every day, we are putting all kinds of foods and drinks into our digestive system. Despite our precautions, sometimes harmful germs like bacteria or viruses manage to gain entry, too. The gut has several defenses against germs, such as the strong acid in the stomach. Occasionally the germs survive, and they begin to multiply in the gut. The result is a digestive infection. It may pass in a few hours or become life-threatening, depending on which germs cause it and the body's resistance and general health.

Most cases of "upset stomach" are due to gastroenteritis. This means inflammation of the stomach and intestines, and it is often caused by viruses. Sometimes it is accompanied by vomiting and/or diarrhea. The viruses can spread from one person to another by body contact, such as shaking hands – they do not have to be in the food itself. Generally, the symptoms are abdominal pain, diarrhea and nausea (feeling sick), and they fade in about two days.

Poor food hygiene also helps infections to spread. Germs can spread from people's hands or cooking utensils onto the foods. Unless the foods are cooked thoroughly, or peeled or washed if they are raw, the germs are then taken in with the food.

Salmonella bacteria may be present in some foods, such as chicken or eggs and especially pork. If the food is not properly cooked, they can get into the gut and breed there, causing pain, diarrhea and a raised temperature. People who are otherwise healthy can usually fight off the infection, although it may be more serious in young children and the elderly.

In many parts of the world, serious gut infections like dysentery, cholera and typhoid are common and cause much suffering. They produce severe pain and diarrhea. The body loses large quantities of water and mineral salts, and becomes dehydrated. Sufferers need to take in plenty of clean water and salts to replace those that have been lost. However, in some areas the water supply is not clean, but is contaminated by sewage. The bacteria pass into the water from feces, and are taken in again when contaminated water is used for drinking, cooking or washing.

Sometimes, what seems like gastroenteritis does not involve infection by germs. Other conditions produce similar symptoms. They include allergy to certain foods, poisons in the food, eating too much rich or spicy food or too much alcohol.

▽ Richer countries can afford to treat water to make sure it is clean, and dispose of sewage safely and without contamination. Poor countries may lack the money to build and run the expensive water-treatment and sewage plants.

Nutrient transport

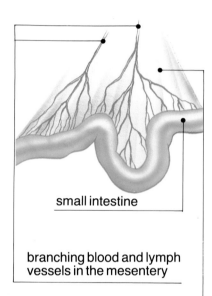

small intestine

branching blood and lymph vessels in the mesentery

folded sheet of mesentery attached along intestine

△ Spread out, the mesentery is a long, fan-shaped sheet of tissue with the intestine set into its edge. It supports the blood and lymph vessels running to and from the intestine. In the body, it is folded and packed into the abdomen.

When nutrients have been absorbed from the intestines, they must be transported to the places in the body where they are needed. The blood does this job, flowing endlessly around the body, pumped by the heart.

The gut needs a blood supply for its own purposes, bringing the oxygen and nutrients to its own tissues. Arteries carry blood to each region of the gut, as they do for other body organs. Several gastric arteries go to the stomach, while the rectal arteries supply the rectum.

Veins usually return "used" blood straight to the heart, after its oxygen and nutrients have been used by the tissues. However, blood leaving the small and large intestines is loaded with dissolved nutrients, which it has absorbed from the digested foods. Most of these nutrients need to be taken to the liver, for alteration and storage. So the veins leaving the intestines join to form one large vessel, the **portal vein**, which goes to the liver. This blood eventually leaves the liver as usual, flowing to the heart along the hepatic veins.

The arteries and veins supplying the intestines do not lie loose and floppy in the abdomen. They are embedded in a large sheet of tissue called the **mesentery**, which anchors the intestine to the back inside wall of the abdomen. The mesentery is tightly folded around the various loops of intestines. It holds them in place so that they do not get tangled and knotted as they squirm with the movements of peristalsis.

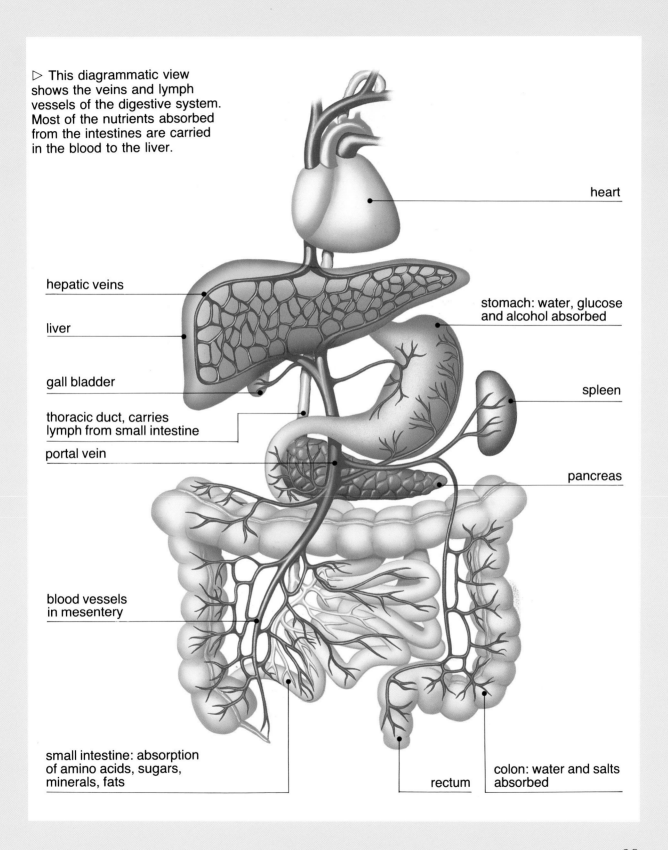

▷ This diagrammatic view shows the veins and lymph vessels of the digestive system. Most of the nutrients absorbed from the intestines are carried in the blood to the liver.

heart

hepatic veins

liver

gall bladder

thoracic duct, carries lymph from small intestine

portal vein

stomach: water, glucose and alcohol absorbed

spleen

pancreas

blood vessels in mesentery

small intestine: absorption of amino acids, sugars, minerals, fats

rectum

colon: water and salts absorbed

39

The many functions of the liver

The liver is the largest gland in the body, weighing about 1.5 kilograms (3 lb). It is also central to many aspects of body chemistry. So far, we know that it plays a role in more than 500 different chemical pathways. There are certainly many more as yet undiscovered.

The liver is a type of "chemical factory." That is, it deals with the many nutrients absorbed from the intestines. The nutrients arrive in "used" blood along the portal vein. In addition, the liver has its own supply from the hepatic artery.

▽ The liver is in the upper right of the abdomen, about level with the upper arm (below right). It has two "inputs," in the form of two blood supplies, and two "outputs," one as used blood and one as bile for the intestines.

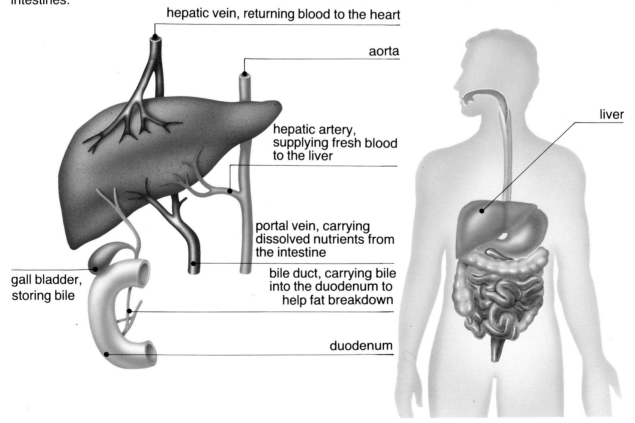

hepatic vein, returning blood to the heart

aorta

liver

hepatic artery, supplying fresh blood to the liver

portal vein, carrying dissolved nutrients from the intestine

gall bladder, storing bile

bile duct, carrying bile into the duodenum to help fat breakdown

duodenum

When the nutrients reach the liver, some are broken down still further. Certain amino acids, the building blocks of proteins, are split to make energy-giving materials. A by-product of this process is urea, a waste material that passes out in the urine. Other amino acids are joined together and built up into small proteins, which are carried off in the blood for use around the body. Substances which help the blood to clot are also produced here.

Large quantities of the sugar, **glucose**, are formed by breakdown of carbohydrates and absorbed during digestion. Glucose is the body's main short-term energy source, since it can be used quickly to give rapid bursts of energy. But not all the glucose can be used at once. Some needs to be stored as a medium-term reserve, for the times when no food is being digested. So the liver joins thousands of glucose molecules to make much larger starch-like molecules known as **glycogen**. Some glycogen is stored in the liver and some in muscles and other tissues.

Quantities of fats are also stored in the liver. These are broken down more slowly to provide energy and form a long-term energy reserve.

Red blood cells only live for about three months, then they become old, worn-out and useless. Several organs, including the liver, help to break them down and reuse some of their molecules. Iron, in particular, is an important part of red blood cells and is stored in the liver for future use. The liver also makes bile fluid, and keeps a supply of various vitamins.

Yet other functions of the liver concern harmful substances like alcohol and certain other drugs. The liver breaks these down and makes them harmless; a process called "detoxification."

▽ The cells from a diseased liver under the light microscope. The condition shown here is cirrhosis, in which the normal smooth texture of the liver is broken up by bands of fibrous tissue, colored in blue (see also page 42). Cirrhosis has many causes, including drinking too much alcohol.

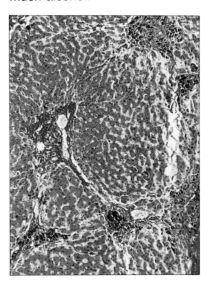

Inside the liver

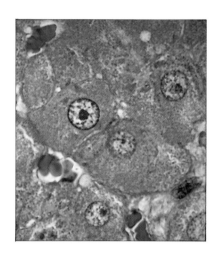

△ The light microscope reveals individual liver cells. Each cell is joined into a group and bounded by a thin blue outline, and has a big nucleus, or control center. One nucleus shows up as a pale circle with a red spot, near the center of the photograph. Liver cells are large, as cells go. Compare them with the red blood cells, which are the small, bright red circles squeezing through capillaries between the groups of liver cells.

The liver has an enormous range of functions. Yet its structure looks very simple, at least to the unaided eye. This organ is deep red in color, has a soft texture, and lies mainly on the right side of the body, on a level with the stomach. It is divided into a small left lobe, and a much larger right lobe which has the gall bladder beneath it. The liver has a very large blood supply. About 1.5 liters or quarts of blood flow through it every minute.

Under a microscope, liver tissue is seen to be built up of relatively simple units called lobules. These are flat sheets of roughly cube-shaped liver cells, termed hepatocytes. The hepatocytes all look much the same, despite the liver's hundreds of chemical roles. The sheets of hepatocytes are arranged so that they fan out from a central tiny vein. Between the sheets are spaces through which blood flows. Each lobule is six-sided and 1 to 3 millimeters (0.2 in) across.

Between the lobules are tiny branches of the portal vein, the hepatic artery and the hepatic ducts. The portal vein brings nutrients from digestion. The hepatic artery carries oxygen-rich blood direct from the heart. The hepatic or bile ducts collect bile and channel it along another tube, the cystic duct, to the gall bladder.

The tiny veins in the center of each lobule join to form the hepatic veins. These large vessels convey "used" blood, loaded with many products of liver chemistry, back to the heart.

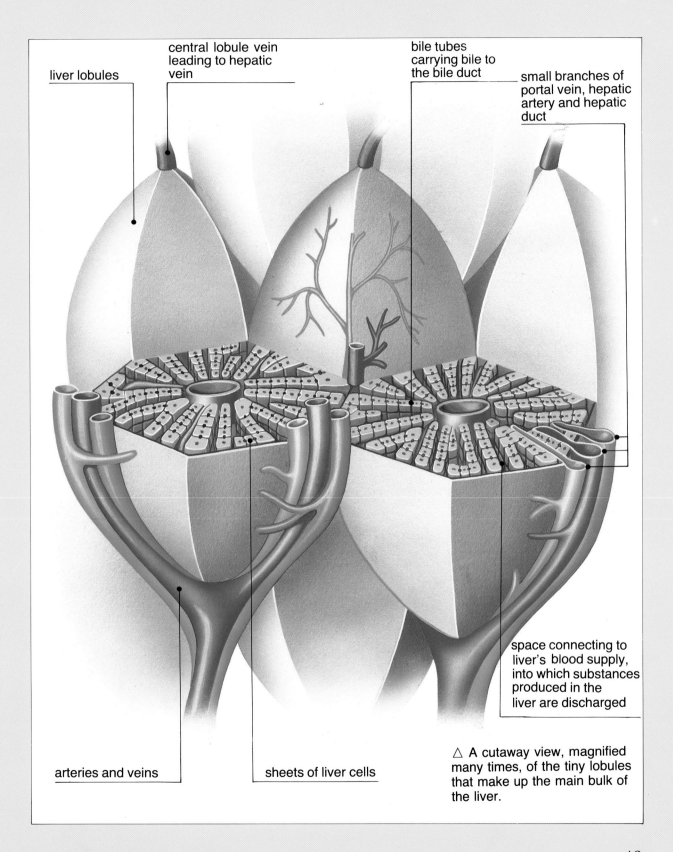

liver lobules

central lobule vein leading to hepatic vein

bile tubes carrying bile to the bile duct

small branches of portal vein, hepatic artery and hepatic duct

space connecting to liver's blood supply, into which substances produced in the liver are discharged

arteries and veins

sheets of liver cells

△ A cutaway view, magnified many times, of the tiny lobules that make up the main bulk of the liver.

43

Too much and too little

We grow enough food on our planet to feed all the people on it. It is estimated that, from the basic foodstuffs we are producing today, we could provide a healthy diet for everyone – and still feed many more people. But across the globe, millions of people are starving and dying because they do not have enough to eat. Millions more suffer because their diet is not varied and balanced. And yet, millions become ill and die because they eat too much, especially fatty things such as fried foods and dairy products. They have "diseases of affluence," like obesity and heart problems.

▽ The diagram below compares food production (pink bars) with the number of people (blue bars), for each main region of the world. For example, in Africa about 11 percent of the world's people are trying to survive on 7 percent of its food. The result is disease, famine and millions of lives lost.

━🍲 food production

🧍 population

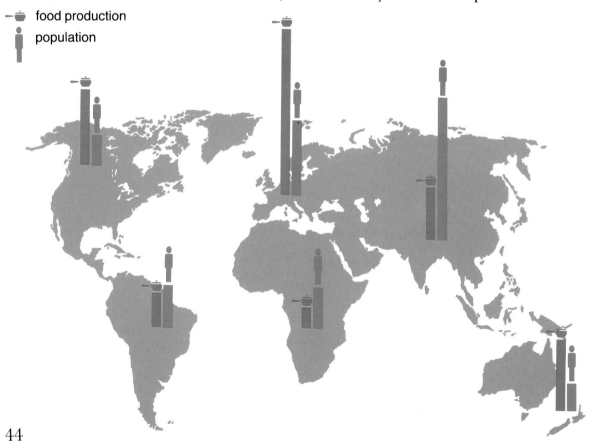

△ Many millions of people in the richer, developed countries take food for granted. We can choose from a huge variety of things to eat.

◁ Many millions of people in the poorer, less developed nations have a daily struggle simply to find enough food to eat. This Ethiopian mother has been treating her child with oral rehydration therapy (page 35). But every day, hundreds of other children die from hunger and infection around the globe. We have enough food for every human body in the world, but we do not distribute it properly.

45

Glossary

Alkali: a substance that can neutralize an acid, making it inactive. There are alkaline conditions in the duodenum which neutralize stomach acid.

Amino acids: the basic building blocks that make up proteins. Foods containing protein are broken down into their amino acids during digestion.

Amylase: an enzyme present in saliva and pancreatic juice. It digests starch into sugar, which can then be absorbed.

Anus: the opening at the end of the digestive system through which feces are discharged.

Appendix: a finger-sized projection at the beginning of the colon. Sometimes it becomes inflamed, causing appendicitis.

Balanced diet: eating food that contains the correct proportions of the main dietary substances, for good health.

Bile: a greenish liquid produced in the liver and stored in the gallbladder. It is passed into the duodenum to help in the breakdown of fat into small globules that can be absorbed.

Capillaries: tiny blood vessels penetrating every organ of the body, and connecting arteries to veins. Capillary walls are very thin, so small food molecules can pass through them and enter the bloodstream.

Carbohydrates: food substances that provide energy. Sugars and starches are carbohydrates. Bread is a rich source.

Chyme: the semi-liquid contents of the gut after it leaves the stomach. It comprises partly digested food material, digestive juices and mucus.

Chymotrypsin: an enzyme found in pancreatic juice which digests protein.

Colon: the main part of the large intestine. Wide part of the gut in which water and mineral salts are reabsorbed from digested food remains to produce semi-solid feces.

Digestive system: the parts of the body specialized for taking in, breaking down and absorbing food. It consists of the gut, liver, pancreas and other organs.

Duodenum: the short section of the small intestine leading from the stomach. The pancreas and bile duct pour their secretions into the duodenum

Enzyme: a substance which causes the breakdown or digestion of food material. Enzymes remain unchanged after this process.

Esophagus: the gullet; the section of gut carrying food from the mouth to the stomach.

Feces: semi-solid waste material remaining after digestion. Consists principally of indigestible material and the remains of bacteria living in the gut, mucus, and rubbed-off gut wall.

Fat: a greasy substance, which may be a solid or an oil. Fat is a long-term energy source and is stored in the body.

Fiber: indigestible plant material, forming an important part of the diet. Fiber adds bulk to the feces, preventing constipation as well as disorders of the lower gut.

Fundus: the broad upper part of the stomach, where food is stored temporarily.

Glucose: a form of sugar which can be broken down to release energy.

Glycogen: the form in which carbohydrate is stored in the body. It can be rapidly broken down into glucose when energy is needed.

Gut: the long tube extending from mouth to anus, making up the digestive tract.

Hormone: a chemical messenger produced by a gland and released into the blood, which carries it so that the hormone can provide instructions to another part of the body.

Hydrochloric acid: the strong acid secreted into the stomach, where it provides proper conditions to start the digestion of protein. Hydrochloric acid is neutralized by the alkaline conditions in the duodenum.

Insulin: a hormonal substance produced in the pancreas and released directly into the blood. It regulates the amount of sugar in the blood, and its lack causes diabetes.

Intestine: the length of gut between the stomach and anus, comprising small intestine, large intestine and rectum.

Lymph: a milky liquid

circulated in the lymph system. Lymph resembles blood from which all the red cells have been filtered. Lymph carries fat absorbed from the intestines.

Mesentery: thin sheet of tissue, with many blood vessels, which supports the gut in the abdomen, supplies it with blood, and carries digested nutrients away in the bloodstream to the liver.

Microvilli: finger-like projections on the cells which make up the surface of the villi, increasing the area of the gut lining still further.

Minerals: substances used in building bones, teeth and many other parts of the body. Minerals are not broken down but are absorbed unchanged from food in the gut.

Mucosa: the inner lining of the gut, containing glands.

Mucus: a slippery, watery material produced from the mucosa. It protects the gut and lubricates waste passing through the colon and rectum.

Nutrient: a food substance, used by the body for building or repair of tissues, or for energy.

Pancreas: a gland which secretes a mixture of enzymes into the duodenum. Also secretes insulin into the blood.

Pepsin: an enzyme produced in the stomach, which begins the digestion of protein.

Pepsinogen: a substance released from the stomach wall and changed into the enzyme pepsin by the action of hydrochloric acid.

Peristalsis: the wave-like muscular movement of the walls of the whole digestive system, which carries food along.

Portal vein: the blood vessel which carries absorbed nutrients from the intestine to the liver.

Protein: food substances derived from meat and from some vegetables, nuts and cereals. Important in building new body tissues.

Pylorus: the lower part of the stomach, in which food is mixed and churned, and digestion of protein begins.

Rectum: the last part of the large intestine. Short length of gut in which feces are temporarily stored before discharge through the anus.

Sphincter: a ring of muscle, acting as a valve to control the flow of material through the gut.

Starch: a form of carbohydrate derived from plant materials. Must be turned into sugar through digestion before it can be used by the body.

Submucosa: the middle layer of the gut wall, between the mucosa and muscle layers.

Sugars: mostly sweet-tasting carbohydrates. Obtained mainly from plant materials, and used in the body to supply energy.

Trypsin: a protein-digesting enzyme in pancreatic juice.

Villi: tiny finger-like projections covering the lining of the small intestine through which nutrients are absorbed. Villi increase the area of the gut lining, making food absorption more efficient.

Vitamins: organic substances found in food in very tiny quantities, which are essential for good health.

Index